THERE IS
BEAUTY TO BE FOUND
IN THE
MIDDLE OF THE MESS

Undone
IS BEAUTIFUL

Journal

Belle City Gifts
Racine, Wisconsin, USA

Belle City Gifts is an imprint of BroadStreet Publishing Group LLC.
Broadstreetpublishing.com

Undone Is Beautiful
© 2015 by Michele Cushatt

ISBN 978-1-4245-5160-6

Design by Chris Garborg I www.garborgdesign.com
Editorial services by Michelle Winger I www.literallyprecise.com

Printed in China.

15   16   17   18   19   20   21     7   6   5   4   3   2   1

Let the one who is
thirsty come, and let
the one who wishes
take the free gift of
the water of life.

Revelation 22:17 NIV

# INTRODUCTION

When I sat in high school English class doodling in my pink spiral notebook, I never imagined my life would turn out as it did. I saw the future in only happy hues—happily-ever-afters and dreams come true.

But real life didn't end up quite as perfect as I imagined it. It never does. I'm guessing you already know this. So what do we do when life doesn't go according to plan?

We could unravel, sinking into fear, bitterness, and despair: an understandable response to the unfairness of life. But raging against reality doesn't do a thing to change it. And despair can be a deep hole to dig out of. I know.

What if it's possible to find a tangible, calming peace that transcends circumstances? I believe it is. But it requires an intentional shift in perspective.

That's what this journal is about. As I navigated my own undone life—a complicated marriage, painful seasons of parenting, and a life-threatening illness three times over—I discovered I needed more than shallow platitudes and cheap clichés. I needed to know I wasn't alone. I needed concrete evidence that God was both with me and for me.

That's when I started a journal. Each morning I pulled out my Bible and opened to a fresh journal page. Then I wrote the date at the top, asking God for evidence of his activity in the middle of my undone story. It didn't take long for him to answer. And the results stunned me. Not only did I begin to see his affection toward me and presence with me in tangible ways, I also experienced peace. Sweet, soul-healing peace. My circumstances hadn't changed, but my heart had.

The same can be true for you, my friend. Whatever your story, whatever the details of your undone life, it's possible to make peace with it, to find the beauty hidden within. God loves you more than you know. Look for him, and let him surprise you.

Undone *is* beautiful.

*Michele Cushatt*

BE KIND TO ONE ANOTHER, TENDER-HEARTED, FORGIVING EACH OTHER,

JUST AS GOD IN CHRIST ALSO HAS FORGIVEN YOU.

EPHESIANS 4:32 NASB

Forgiveness, of the authentic and true kind, is a rare find. We spend years restoring worn antiques, hundreds of dollars repairing wrecked and dented cars. But if a relationship sustains damage, we're more likely to relegate it to the scrap heap than try to restore its shine. We're far more enduring with our valuables than with the people we claim to value (Undone, 40–41).

As God's chosen people, holy and dearly loved, clothe yourselves with compassion, kindness, humility, gentleness and patience.

Colossians 3:12 NIV

A marriage isn't made of lace and pearls, slacks and ties. Nor can it be polished to a perfect shine or wrestled into submission. But it can be built one "I'm sorry," "I forgive you," and "I love you" at a time (Undone, 51).

"THE LORD WILL FIGHT FOR YOU. JUST STAY CALM."

EXODUS 14:14 NLT

*All it took was the presence of Jesus for terror and tension to flee. Not a change in circumstances or a reassurance of how the rest of the story would play out. Not even a solid answer to the question of why. Instead, presence (Undone, 57).*

"HAVE I NOT COMMANDED YOU? BE STRONG AND COURAGEOUS.
DO NOT BE AFRAID; DO NOT BE DISCOURAGED,
FOR THE LORD YOUR GOD WILL BE WITH YOU WHEREVER YOU GO."

JOSHUA 1:9 NIV

Peace isn't a byproduct of control, the payout of a happy conclusion. Peace is the infiltrating, life-giving presence of a very real God (Undone, 57).

"*I* AM THE LORD WHO HEALS YOU."

Exodus 15:26 NLT

From the beginning, my fantasy of a perfect life was just that—a fantasy. It grew from the innocent and untried imagination of a girl who wanted her life to read like a fairytale. But I'd forgotten that even fairytales have villains and hardships and unexpected twists in plots. I kept holding out for my happy ending, but missed the fact that I'd already received it. A hero who pushed past my fear with the reassurance of his very real presence (Undone, 57).

*I* KNOW THE LORD IS ALWAYS WITH ME.

I WILL NOT BE SHAKEN,

FOR HE IS RIGHT BESIDE ME.

PSALM 16:8 NLT

God created. God blessed. God rejected. God mourned.
God promised. God loved. God gave. God healed. God rescued.
God redeemed. God will come again! (Undone, 60)

You will make known to me the path of life;

In Your presence is fullness of joy;

In Your right hand there are pleasures forever.

Psalm 16:11 NASB

Peace has always been a person. The presence of God in the form of a child, sent from the perfection of heaven to an earth wrecked with pain, so the life we'd always dreamed of—heaven—could be accessible to us (Undone, 62).

*Some trust in chariots and some in horses,*

*but we trust in the name of the Lord our God.*

*They collapse and fall, but we rise and stand upright.*

Psalm 20:7–8 ESV

*Flimsy belief gives birth to fear, not courage (Undone, 70).*

THE LORD IS MY SHEPHERD, I LACK NOTHING.

HE MAKES ME LIE DOWN IN GREEN PASTURES,

HE LEADS ME BESIDE QUIET WATERS,

HE REFRESHES MY SOUL.

PSALM 23:1-2 NIV

*I could either hang on to fear or hold on to my faith. But I could not hang on to both (Undone, 70).*

HE WILL HIDE ME IN HIS SHELTER IN THE DAY OF TROUBLE;

HE WILL CONCEAL ME UNDER THE COVER OF HIS TENT;

HE WILL LIFT ME HIGH UPON A ROCK.

PSALM 27:5 ESV

It's a difficult tension, living with one hand embracing earth and the other reaching for the eternal. To think only of heaven is to miss out on the gift of life. And to dwell on this life is to miss out on the grandeur—and anticipation—of what is yet to come. Instead, I needed to see heaven and earth through the lens of the other. Only then could I embrace the glorious hues of both (Undone, 71).

GOD IS OUR REFUGE AND STRENGTH,

A VERY PRESENT HELP IN TROUBLE.

THEREFORE WE WILL NOT FEAR,

THOUGH THE EARTH SHOULD CHANGE

AND THOUGH THE MOUNTAINS SLIP INTO THE HEART OF THE SEA.

PSALM 46:1-2 NASB

I'd been given the gift of a single life, one I was to embrace, celebrate, and receive with joy. But the end of the gift was never meant to be the end of the story. Only the beginning of one (Undone, 71).

BLESSED ARE THOSE WHOSE STRENGTH IS IN YOU,

WHOSE HEARTS ARE SET ON PILGRIMAGE.

AS THEY PASS THROUGH THE VALLEY OF BAKA,

THEY MAKE IT A PLACE OF SPRINGS;

THE AUTUMN RAINS ALSO COVER IT WITH POOLS.

THEY GO FROM STRENGTH TO STRENGTH,

TILL EACH APPEARS BEFORE GOD IN ZION.

PSALM 84:5-7 NIV

*Authenticity ministers far more than put-togetherness. And vulnerability builds a far stronger bond than perfection (Undone, 82).*

*Those who go to the God Most High for safety
will be protected by the Almighty.
I will say to the Lord, "You are my place of safety and protection.
You are my God and I trust you."*

Psalm 91:1-2 NCV

There is strength in empty. Not the kind of strength we wish for. We want polished strength, the kind that wears a cape and leaps tall buildings with a single bound. I couldn't leap or fly or save anyone from catastrophe. In fact, I could barely show up. But I did. Show up. And that ended up being a strength all of its own (Undone, 82).

He will cover you with his feathers,

and under his wings you can hide.

His truth will be your shield and protection.

PSALM 91:4 NCV

Ministry—of the truest kind—isn't about impressing unknown strangers with spotless presentations and a flawless life. It's about exposing the hidden imperfections and giving others permission to do the same. Becoming a fellow struggler who delivers zero judgment but abundant grace (Undone, 82).

*To him who is able to keep you from falling, and to make you stand without blemish in the presence of his glory with rejoicing, to the only God our Savior, through Jesus Christ our Lord, be glory, majesty, power, and authority, before all time and now and forever. Amen.*

JUDE 24-25 NRSV

Few things display unadulterated beauty like a pouring out when you've nothing to give (Undone, 83).

You NEED NOT BE AFRAID OF SUDDEN DISASTER
OR THE DESTRUCTION THAT COMES UPON THE WICKED,
FOR THE LORD IS YOUR SECURITY.
HE WILL KEEP YOUR FOOT FROM BEING CAUGHT IN A TRAP.

PROVERBS 3:25-26 NLT

Worry, like cancer, consumes life, eating away at a person from the inside out. It exaggerates the unknown and clouds the known until the worried person sees only the horror of what might be, rather than the beauty of what already is (Undone, 92).

GOOD SENSE MAKES ONE SLOW TO ANGER,
AND IT IS TO HIS GLORY TO OVERLOOK AN OFFENSE.

PROVERBS 19:11 ESV

Motherhood is more than posed and frame-able moments. It's not the sum of blissful images filling the pages of a scrapbook. A mother is made in the difficult, challenging, and very real crises that never make it to a page (Undone, 102).

*E*VERY WORD OF GOD IS FLAWLESS:

HE IS A SHIELD TO THOSE WHO TAKE REFUGE IN HIM.

PROVERBS 30:5 NIV

Now, when I look at the family portrait on the mantel,
I no longer see flaws and the many ways I failed.
I see a story taking shape behind the scenes (Undone, 102).

He has made everything beautiful in its time. Also He has put eternity in their hearts, except that no one can find out the work that God does from beginning to end.

Ecclesiastes 3:11 NKJV

Want a life rich with joy? Spend yourself. Desire fullness from head to toe? Find someone to feed. Looking for a life that shines— turns dark into light? Find a need and meet it (Undone, 132).

Unto us a Child is born,

Unto us a Son is given:

And the government will be upon His shoulder.

And His name will be called

Wonderful, Counselor, Mighty God,

Everlasting Father, Prince of Peace.

Isaiah 9:6 NKJV

*The life of a true Jesus-follower—someone who both says and means her promise of "anywhere" and "anything"—doesn't follow smooth, paved roads (Undone, 134).*

"See, God has come to save me.

I will trust in him and not be afraid.

The Lord God is my strength and my song;

he has given me victory."

ISAIAH 12:2

*The only way to find the life I always wanted was to let the lesser life go (Undone, 134).*

YOU WILL KEEP IN PERFECT PEACE
THOSE WHOSE MINDS ARE STEADFAST,

BECAUSE THEY TRUST IN YOU.

ISAIAH 26:3 NIV

*Sometimes messy is the necessary beginning
to the makings of extraordinary (Undone, 137).*

O LORD, YOU WILL ORDAIN PEACE FOR US,

FOR INDEED, ALL THAT WE HAVE DONE, YOU HAVE DONE FOR US.

ISAIAH 26:12 NRSV

*It is in the less than idyllic moments that a family is made*
*(Undone, 139).*

$\mathcal{I}$N REPENTANCE AND REST IS YOUR SALVATION,

IN QUIETNESS AND TRUST IS YOUR STRENGTH.

ISAIAH 30:15 NIV

*There is strength in the person who digs deep to both disagree and love with equal passion. To make convictions known, maybe even say goodbye. But who, at the end of all the tough decisions, has the guts to say, "I love you. And that won't ever change" (Undone, 145).*

Don't be afraid, for I am with you. Don't be discouraged, for I am your God. I will strengthen you and help you. I will hold you up with my victorious right hand.

Isaiah 41:10 NLT

*No matter how much time you have, it's never quite enough*
*(Undone, 155).*

I, THE LORD YOUR GOD, HOLD YOUR RIGHT HAND; IT IS I WHO SAY TO YOU,

"FEAR NOT, I AM THE ONE WHO HELPS YOU."

ISAIAH 41:13 ESV

Cancer, as heinous and evil as it was, had delivered an unexpected gift. It taught us how to live. It taught me the immeasurable value of today (Undone, 157).

When you go through deep waters, I will be with you.
When you go through rivers of difficulty, you will not drown.
When you walk through the fire of oppression, you will not be burned up;
the flames will not consume you. For I am the Lord, your God,
the Holy One of Israel, your Savior.

Isaiah 43:2-3 NLT

Faith isn't rooted in the past or the future. It's birthed in how we approach and handle today. It's the anchor that holds us firmly in this moment, allowing us the freedom to experience it and enjoy it, regardless of the regrets and what-ifs (Undone, 157).

Do not call to mind the former things, Or ponder things of the past.

"Behold, I will do something new. Now it will spring forth;

Will you not be aware of it?

I will even make a roadway in the wilderness,

Rivers in the desert."

ISAIAH 43:18-19 NASB

Just because something is hard doesn't mean we're not called to it. And just because it's hard doesn't mean it's not good. God left the comfort of heaven for a complicated, uncomfortable human life. The world has never seen a calling more difficult. Nor a calling more good. The sacrifice required to redeem a life. The light offered in the darkness (Undone, 169).

*Can a woman forget her nursing child,*

*or show no compassion for the child of her womb?*

*Even these may forget, yet I will not forget you.*

*See, I have inscribed you on the palms of my hands;*

*your walls are continually before me.*

ISAIAH 49:15-16 NRSV

*Moments between mother and child aren't ordinary.*
*They're sacred (Undone, 177).*

THE LORD IS NEAR TO ALL WHO CALL ON HIM,

TO ALL WHO CALL ON HIM IN TRUTH.

PSALM 145:18 NIV

What happens between a mother and child, or father and child,
gives an infant, a child, a sense of who they are in connection to
someone else. Although individual and unique, a child can grow
into that individuality only through the security of connection
(Undone, 177).

*T*HOUGH THE MOUNTAINS BE SHAKEN

AND THE HILLS BE REMOVED,

YET MY UNFAILING LOVE FOR YOU WILL NOT BE SHAKEN

NOR MY COVENANT OF PEACE BE REMOVED,"

SAYS THE LORD, WHO HAS COMPASSION ON YOU.

ISAIAH 54:10 NIV

*It is in relationship with significant others that a child gains a sense of who he is apart (Undone, 177).*

*If* you pour yourself out for the hungry

and satisfy the desire of the afflicted,

then shall your light rise in the darkness

and your gloom be as the noonday.

Isaiah 58:10 ESV

The cross: the single most significant and foolhardy investment of all time. A sacrificial offering, made once for all, for a people who'd never appreciate the cost. People who would scoff at it only moments after receipt. And what for? To help an unmoored people know they had a place to anchor (*Undone*, 180).

"To give them beauty for ashes,

The oil of joy for mourning,

The garment of praise for the spirit of heaviness;

That they may be called trees of righteousness,

The planting of the Lord, that He may be glorified."

Isaiah 61:3 NKJV

*True independence finds its anchor in relationship (Undone, 181).*

"WHERE YOUR TREASURE IS, THERE YOUR HEART WILL BE ALSO."

Matthew 6:21 NASB

*Wounds suffered in relationships are also healed in relationship. That's both the rub and the beauty of it. The very thing that brought us pain will be the means through which our healing will come (Undone, 181).*

"THEREFORE DO NOT WORRY ABOUT TOMORROW, FOR TOMORROW WILL WORRY ABOUT ITSELF. EACH DAY HAS ENOUGH TROUBLE OF ITS OWN."

MATTHEW 6:34 NIV

*When human love fails, a greater love remains.*
*A healing, filling, securing love (Undone, 182).*

"ARE NOT TWO SPARROWS SOLD FOR A PENNY?
AND NOT ONE OF THEM WILL FALL TO THE GROUND APART FROM YOUR FATHER.
BUT EVEN THE HAIRS OF YOUR HEAD ARE ALL NUMBERED."

MATTHEW 10:29-30 ESV

*Perfectionism isn't rational. It's poison (Undone, 187).*

"WHOEVER FINDS THEIR LIFE WILL LOSE IT,

AND WHOEVER LOSES THEIR LIFE FOR MY SAKE WILL FIND IT."

MATTHEW 10:39 NIV

*Parenting is easy before you become a parent (Undone, 187).*

"COME TO ME, ALL YOU WHO ARE WEARY AND CARRY HEAVY BURDENS, AND I WILL GIVE YOU REST."

MATTHEW 11:28 NLT

Only a marred life gives birth to the most beautiful redemption (Undone, 190).

"WHO OF YOU BY WORRYING CAN ADD A SINGLE HOUR TO YOUR LIFE?"

LUKE 12:25 NIV

Just as a writer must embrace a rough draft as the necessary means to a book's successful end, I had to learn how to embrace my life's process. Including the countless ways my shortcomings and flaws have made me a better character in my own story (Undone, 190).

"I WILL NOT LEAVE YOU AS ORPHANS; I WILL COME TO YOU."

JOHN 14:18 NIV

*Life must be lived with a writer's courage. Just as a blank page cannot be improved, nothing can be done with an unlived, untried life (Undone, 190).*

"I AM LEAVING YOU WITH A GIFT—PEACE OF MIND AND HEART. AND THE PEACE I GIVE IS A GIFT THE WORLD CANNOT GIVE. SO DON'T BE TROUBLED OR AFRAID."

JOHN 14:27 NLT

To dare to live will involve mistakes and missteps. We will end up with choices we regret, opportunities we missed, words we wish we could go back and say or leave unsaid. Perfection is impossible. But a rough draft, no matter how flawed, sits within reach of an artist's redemption (Undone, 191).

"I HAVE TOLD YOU THESE THINGS, SO THAT IN ME YOU MAY HAVE PEACE. IN THIS WORLD YOU WILL HAVE TROUBLE. BUT TAKE HEART! I HAVE OVERCOME THE WORLD."

JOHN 16:33 NIV

This is the grace—the holiness—of a rough-draft life. Of children who struggle and parents who fail. Of broken marriages and disappointing A-minuses. Of trying and stumbling, but finding the grace to get up and try again (Undone, 191)

"THIS IS ETERNAL LIFE: THAT THEY KNOW YOU, THE ONLY TRUE GOD,
AND JESUS CHRIST, WHOM YOU HAVE SENT."

JOHN 17:3 NIV

*This is a rough-draft life. And whatever I didn't like about today, I can always edit tomorrow (Undone, 192).*

Then, the same day at evening, being the first day of the week, when the doors were shut where the disciples were assembled, for fear of the Jews, Jesus came and stood in the midst, and said to them, "Peace be with you."

JOHN 20:19 NKJV

A boat anchored to itself is not anchored at all (Undone, 201).

YOU ARE MY HIDING PLACE;

YOU SHALL PRESERVE ME FROM TROUBLE;

YOU SHALL SURROUND ME WITH SONGS OF DELIVERANCE.

PSALM 32:7 NKJV

*Shoring up your faith in the right place is far more important than simply claiming to have it. If I believe only in what I can see, manage, and control, sooner or later something will come along to rock my boat (Undone, 201).*

WE ALSO HAVE JOY WITH OUR TROUBLES, BECAUSE WE KNOW THAT THESE
TROUBLES PRODUCE PATIENCE. AND PATIENCE PRODUCES CHARACTER, AND
CHARACTER PRODUCES HOPE.

ROMANS 5:3-4 NCV

We must secure our faith where it cannot be unmoored: in the one who controls the waves and whose peace runs so deep we find a way to sleep in the storm (Undone, 201).

THE LORD ALWAYS KEEPS HIS PROMISES;

HE IS GRACIOUS IN ALL HE DOES.

PSALM 145:13 NLT

_Faith is choosing the anchor of your focus. It's about turning your eyes away from the questions that lead to fear, and instead locking eyes with the one who knows the answers (Undone, 202)._

I AM SURE THAT NEITHER DEATH, NOR LIFE, NOR ANGELS, NOR RULING SPIRITS, NOTHING NOW, NOTHING IN THE FUTURE, NO POWERS, NOTHING ABOVE US, NOTHING BELOW US, NOR ANYTHING ELSE IN THE WHOLE WORLD WILL EVER BE ABLE TO SEPARATE US FROM THE LOVE OF GOD THAT IS IN CHRIST JESUS OUR LORD.

ROMANS 8:38-39 NCV

*Allowing yourself frailty is one of the kindest things you can do for yourself (Undone, 209).*

*I urge you, brothers and sisters, in view of God's mercy, to offer your bodies as a living sacrifice, holy and pleasing to God—this is your true and proper worship. Do not conform to the pattern of this world, but be transformed by the renewing of your mind. Then you will be able to test and approve what God's will is—his good, pleasing and perfect will.*

ROMANS 12:1-2 NIV

*Life is far more beautiful—and endurable—*
*when you don't have to do it alone (Undone, 214).*

PRAISE BE TO THE GOD AND FATHER OF OUR LORD JESUS CHRIST, THE FATHER OF COMPASSION AND THE GOD OF ALL COMFORT, WHO COMFORTS US IN ALL OUR TROUBLES, SO THAT WE CAN COMFORT THOSE IN ANY TROUBLE WITH THE COMFORT WE OURSELVES RECEIVE FROM GOD.

2 CORINTHIANS 1:3-4 NIV

In the relinquishing of independence, I discovered community.
My brokenness gave me connection, relationship.
I thought asking for help was an admission of weakness.
Instead, I discovered it a declaration of strength (Undone, 214).

WE HAVE THIS TREASURE IN CLAY JARS, SO THAT IT MAY BE MADE CLEAR THAT THIS EXTRAORDINARY POWER BELONGS TO GOD AND DOES NOT COME FROM US. WE ARE AFFLICTED IN EVERY WAY, BUT NOT CRUSHED; PERPLEXED, BUT NOT DRIVEN TO DESPAIR; PERSECUTED, BUT NOT FORSAKEN; STRUCK DOWN, BUT NOT DESTROYED.

2 CORINTHIANS 4:7-9 NRSV

*Our God is a refuge for the broken, not a shelf for the display of the shiny; no more pride for those who have it all together, or shame for those who don't (Undone, 214).*

So we do not lose heart. Even though our outer nature is wasting away, our inner nature is being renewed day by day. For this slight momentary affliction is preparing us for an eternal weight of glory beyond all measure, because we look not at what can be seen but at what cannot be seen; for what can be seen is temporary, but what cannot be seen is eternal.

2 Corinthians 4:16-18 NRSV

To make peace with a life, to see it as art, requires a stepping back. Only then do we see boats bobbing on the waves and a new sun rising in the sky. Spontaneity and randomness show evidence of artistic design. Though appearing undone, it hints that imperfection could turn into the makings of an incredible story. And perhaps a breathtaking work of art (Undone, 221).

For this reason I am happy when I have weaknesses, insults, hard times, sufferings, and all kinds of troubles for Christ. Because when I am weak, then I am truly strong.

2 Corinthians 12:10 NCV

In my attempts to manage my life,
I missed out on the vibrancy of it (Undone, 222).

*For I am confident of this very thing, that He who began a good work in you will perfect it until the day of Christ Jesus.*

Philippians 1:6 NASB

Only in grieving could I free myself to keep living. Against all odds, I started to see the flaws as a necessary part of the canvas of my story. Then, only then, did I begin to make peace (Undone, 223).

# Our citizenship is in heaven.

Philippians 3:20 NIV

A story is more than a neat and tidy house with all the laundry done and dishes put away. And a life is more than the limit of my efforts. A real family—a well-lived life—is found in the marker on the walls, the self-inflicted haircuts, well-used books, children who sometimes make too much noise, and a mom and dad who sometimes lose their patience (Undone, 224).

Don't worry about anything; instead, pray about everything. Tell God what you need, and thank him for all he has done. Then you will experience God's peace, which exceeds anything we can understand. His peace will guard your hearts and minds as you live in Christ Jesus.

Philippians 4:6-7 NLT

Allow yourself to see beyond the chaos to the beautiful story taking shape. One person's mess is another's canvas. It's simply a matter of vantage point (Undone, 224).

LET THE PEACE THAT COMES FROM CHRIST RULE IN YOUR HEARTS. FOR AS MEMBERS OF ONE BODY YOU ARE CALLED TO LIVE IN PEACE. AND ALWAYS BE THANKFUL.

COLOSSIANS 3:15 NLT

*A full life doesn't mean an easy life. In many cases,
it means just the opposite (Undone, 227).*

FAITH IS THE ASSURANCE OF THINGS HOPED FOR,

THE CONVICTION OF THINGS NOT SEEN.

HEBREWS 11:1 ESV

In my wrestling for peace, I'd found a peace that transcends control, that runs deeper and stronger than any assurances or answers. The presence of a God who would see me through (Undone, 231).

*Without faith it is impossible to please God, because anyone who comes to him must believe that he exists and that he rewards those who earnestly seek him.*

HEBREWS 11:6 NIV

*Children—grown-ups—can endure most any horror,*
*as long as they know they're not alone (Undone, pg. 232).*

WHEN TROUBLES OF ANY KIND COME YOUR WAY, CONSIDER IT AN OPPORTUNITY FOR GREAT JOY. FOR YOU KNOW THAT WHEN YOUR FAITH IS TESTED, YOUR ENDURANCE HAS A CHANCE TO GROW.

JAMES 1:2-3 NLT

*Faith in the middle of the unknowns is the only real kind*
*(Undone, 235).*

When people are tempted and still continue strong, they should be happy. After they have proved their faith, God will reward them with life forever. God promised this to all those who love him.

James 1:12 NCV

*Peace can't be found in the past or the future, but only in a Person, and in whom you believe him to be, today (Undone, 235).*

IN ALL THIS YOU GREATLY REJOICE, THOUGH NOW FOR A LITTLE WHILE YOU MAY HAVE HAD TO SUFFER GRIEF IN ALL KINDS OF TRIALS. THESE HAVE COME SO THAT THE PROVEN GENUINENESS OF YOUR FAITH—OF GREATER WORTH THAN GOLD, WHICH PERISHES EVEN THOUGH REFINED BY FIRE—MAY RESULT IN PRAISE, GLORY AND HONOR WHEN JESUS CHRIST IS REVEALED.

1 PETER 1:6-7 NIV

An unexpected life, as difficult and undone as it might be, could end up becoming the life you've been searching for all along (Undone, 235).

He will wipe every tear from their eyes.
Death will be no more;
mourning and crying and pain will be no more,
for the first things have passed away."
And the one who was seated on the throne said,
"See, I am making all things new."

Revelation 21:4-5 NRSV

*Fear has only as much rope as I give it (Undone, 236).*

HUMBLE YOURSELVES THEREFORE UNDER THE MIGHTY HAND OF GOD,
SO THAT HE MAY EXALT YOU IN DUE TIME. CAST ALL YOUR ANXIETY ON HIM,
BECAUSE HE CARES FOR YOU.

1 PETER 5:6-7 NRSV

*Making peace with the unexpected life isn't some trite, Christian cliché. It isn't a beautiful string of words that looks nice and shiny hanging around my neck. The kind of peace that weathers a furious squall by sleeping in the boat is both hard-earned and God-delivered (Undone, 238)*

After you have suffered a little while, the God of all grace, who has called you to his eternal glory in Christ, will himself restore, confirm, strengthen, and establish you.

1 Peter 5:10 ESV

It's an undone life. But I don't have to be undone by it
(Undone, 239).

*Fear not, for I have redeemed you;*
*I have called you by name, you are mine.*

Isaiah 43:1 ESV

This is the choice you and I face each day, as we wrestle with forgiveness and cancer, complicated relationships and unknown outcomes. Retreat or dive? Watch or live? (Undone, 240)

"DO NOT BE AFRAID OR DISCOURAGED BECAUSE OF THIS VAST ARMY.

FOR THE BATTLE IS NOT YOURS, BUT GOD'S."

2 CHRONICLES 20:15 NIV

This is where your story and mine are written, right here with so much at stake and even more possible. And with an incredible Author pulling it all together for the perfect end (Undone, 240).

"I HAVE SWEPT AWAY YOUR OFFENSES LIKE A CLOUD,

YOUR SINS LIKE THE MORNING MIST.

RETURN TO ME,

FOR I HAVE REDEEMED YOU."

ISAIAH 44:22 NIV

Ours is a God who heals all things sick. Who redeems all things lost. Who brings orphans together in unusual families. And who weaves all frail and broken things into a glorious overall whole. A story. His story (Undone, 240).

*I once thought these things were valuable, but now I consider them worthless because of what Christ has done. Yes, everything else is worthless when compared with the infinite value of knowing Christ Jesus my Lord. For his sake I have discarded everything else, counting it all as garbage, so that I could gain Christ.*

PHILIPPIANS 3:7-8 NLT

And the best news of all? When we reach the final page, regardless of what happens between now and then, hope wins (Undone, 240).

# AUTHOR BIO

A storyteller at heart, Michele Cushatt is a wife, mother, author, and speaker who inspires audiences with her characteristic authenticity and warm presence. Her unique style makes you feel like you just spent an afternoon with a good friend, sparking tears one moment and laughter the next.

Michele's speaking experience covers the globe and includes *Women of Faith*, *Compassion International*, *Focus on the Family*, *Proverbs 31*, *Dynamic Communicators International* as well as various radio, video, and audio recording projects. In 2014, she joined Michael Hyatt as his cohost on the popular *This is Your Life* podcast.

Pulling from her unique and dramatic story, Michele's memoir, *Undone: A Story of Making Peace With An Unexpected Life*, released in March 2015.

Michele and her husband, Troy, live in Colorado with their six children, ages 8 to 23. Follow their unfolding story at www.MicheleCushatt.com.